MASTER PIECE
FIRE

Maigen Jones

Table Of Content

Fire

It's what I remember most about my making. There were flames, licking at my face and pouring around my arms. It didn't burn, in fact, I loved the way it changed my body from its chalky clay, to a smooth and shiny vessel. I am lovely, lustrous. Glorious.

The fire stops, and my glistening limbs are pulled from the burning embrace. I remember these hands, they are gentle, loving, a bit scarred in the middle, yet careful still. These are the hands that made me. They know me, and I recognize them.

"You are a masterpiece," he said. His voice akin to honey, his words a promise. He sets me down on a table. I'm facing a small mirror, and for the first time, I'm seeing myself, in a full length of perspective.

I am quite the masterpiece; my body blue like the raging sea, eyes as orange as the setting sun. I speak of these wonders as if I'm familiar with them. Like in another life, I've seen them or known them, but I am brand new. How could I know these things if I have just been made?

"You are my likeness. You've seen what I've seen. Every wonder I've created, it's yours as much as it's mine."

I looked up at the man, puzzled as to how he knew the inner workings of my thoughts. His gentle smile creased his face, his eyes glimmered. "You know what I'm thinking?" I asked.

"I do," he replied, "I know the hearts of all my creations. I breathed the breath of life into each one."

I smiled at him, "You are my creator, The Potter"

"I Am."

"What am I called?"

"You are Eden," the man said.

"And where do I go from here?"

"You are to join my other creations. Go to the village at the base of a mountain, there you will find where you belong."

I thanked The Potter, and hopped from the table. My feet clinked against the wooden floor as I ran for the open door. The wind blew when I reached the threshold. I turned back to him one last time.

"You are a masterpiece," he said once more, "Beautifully, wonderfully, flawlessly made. Do not forget this."

"I won't forget," I said softly. Then I leapt through the door and into the sunshine.

I ran on my feet, I ran with my legs, I ran through grass. The grass is the color green like the fruit of sour apples or an emerald gemstone. My mind raced with many things, these marvels I hadn't seen, yet knew as if they were my own.

I slowed to a walk when I reached the mouth of the village. It was teeming with life; peddlers, merchants, patrons, and musicians pouring through the streets. All of them were glistening just as I did. They were like me, but slightly different.

Some were taller than me, and others were shorter. Some were round, and others slim. Where I was blue, they were red, my orange was their yellow. We were all masterpieces, just like The Potter said.

My stomach ached with hunger, so I wandered into a tavern. Creations danced underneath the candlelight, every table was crowded. The place was bursting with life.

Someone walked up to me and placed a hand on my shoulder, "You must be The Potter's newest creation. What are you called?"

"Eden."

"Welcome, Eden. I'm Meadow. Come, you can sit with me and my friends."

I followed Meadow over to a table in the corner where two other creations sat laughing. They were just as glorious, but they looked different than the other creations I'd seen. Where most bodies were one color, they were multiple. Their eyes were no longer glistening pottery clay, they were large gemstones. Their fingers and toes were drenched in silver and gold.

"I'm Eden," I said, sitting down at the table.

"I'm Lilly, and this is Ravine," one of the creations said.

Ravine smiled at me, then placed her silver-dipped hands on her face, "Do you like my stars?" she asked.

I stared at the glimmering shards embedded on either side of her face. "They're lovely, did The Potter put those on you?"

Ravine, Meadow, and Lilly exchanged a strange look, then Ravine answered, "Our beauty didn't come from The Potter, he made us plain. He created us ordinary when he knew we could be so much more."

"Who told you this?"

"We creations call him Shatter. He takes what The Potter made and changes it, turning us into something even more magnificent." as she said this, the stars in her cheeks began to crumble slightly.

"Shatter can make you magnificent too," Meadow said, wrapping her cracked, golden fingers around my arm.

"The Potter said that I am a masterpiece."

"He lied," Lilly said simply, "He made you ordinary. You could be so much more."

"Come, Shatter will fix you," Ravine whispered.

The three creations stood up and dragged me with them. We left the tavern and traveled to a house at the base of a mountain. It was a shoddy copy of The Potter's house, cracked and sunken with age.

We stepped inside and I instantly felt cold. I wanted to leave, but the three creations seemed so earnest, like they knew something I didn't, and they wanted to help me.

Shatter came around the corner. He was larger than life, just like The Potter, but his eyes lacked The Potter's kindness. When he grabbed me and lifted me onto his table, his hands weren't gentle or loving.

"She wants stars like mine," Ravine said with a grin.

"My golden fingers," Meadow added.

"And give her ruby eyes like mine," Lilly whispered.

Shatter began to work on me, his hands sloppy and rough. He started carving into my cheeks, pouring hot gold over my hands and feet, placing the rubies in my eyes. When he was done, I felt cold and cracked. Ruined.

"You're perfect," the three creations whispered.

I felt...shattered. My ruby eyes made it hard to see, the gold was already beginning to crumble, and the stars were painful. They felt like broken glass against my skin.

I ran.

I ran on my feet, I ran with my legs, I ran through grass. The grass is the color green like the fruit of sour apples or an emerald gemstone.

I ran all the way to The Potter's house on the hill. I burst through the door, and I screamed for him.

"Potter! I'm ruined, please help me."

The Potter sat at his maker's table, he was fashioning something in his hands that I couldn't see.

"You went to see Shatter," he said.

He already knows.

"Please don't be angry with me," I cried. "I met some creations in town. They told me you lied to me. That I am not a masterpiece, that you made me ordinary when I could be so much more, but this–" I wailed, gliding my hands over my body, "This isn't more."

The Potter lifted me onto his table with gentle hands, "When I sent you out into the world, I told you to remember that you are a masterpiece. I've told all my creations this, and while some remember, some begin to forget. They doubt me, they doubt what I have made. And they go to Shatter to "fix" them, but it isn't fixing at all. You saw them, Eden. Their crumbling modifications are nothing compared to the perfection that I fashioned when I made them."

I wiped the tears from my eyes, and sat down on the table, "Can you forgive me?"

The Potter placed a finger beneath my chin, lifting my eyes to his, "You were forgiven long before you were made."

"I cannot stay like this, Potter. Can you heal me?"

He smiled, directing my gaze to his table. There were new pieces resting there, made just for me. My sunset eyes, the ocean in my face, fingers and toes unmarred by crumbling gold.

"Come," The Potter said, "Let's make you whole again."

The gentle hands molded me back to life. I was a masterpiece once again.

It was back into the fire for me, I marveled once again at my glistening form.

When I was done, The Potter sent me out into the world again. The wind blew as it once had, and I turned back to face him.

"You are a masterpiece," he reminded me, "Beautifully, wonderfully, flawlessly made. Do not forget this."

I nodded, and leapt into the sunshine once more.

About the Author

Hi everyone, my name is Maigen Sarina (pronounced sap-pre-na) Jones. Born and raised in Brooklyn New York my birthday is February 5th 1978 My mom named me Maigen after a soap opera character, while the spelling is from dad. He wanted it to be unique and different. He is also responsible for my middle name again, different and unique. It was the name of the game. Jones is our family name. This is a long time coming, dating from 2014. It was never a thought of mine to start writing a book. There are a lot of people and events that are responsible for this phenomenon.

First and foremost, I would like to thank my Lord and Savior, Jesus Christ. I realize that as you read this book that you may find mine believes questionable.

However, everyone has a story to tell. I've lived more than thirty years on this earth, and everyone has a creative and an intelligent way of telling their story.

Welcome to my story, my way, my journey

Made in the USA
Middletown, DE
24 September 2022